Immigrating to Canada? Prepare for Change

A Simple Guide for Prospective Canadian Immigrants

DERVILLE LOWE, MBA

NORWOOD CREATIVE HUB
A Multimedia & Creative Content Design Company
norwood.creativehub@gmail.com

Books by this author are available through booksellers or by contacting:

Derville Lowe
Vancouver, British Columbia, Canada
derville.lowe@gmail.com
1 (250) 899-2961

LOOK FOR INFORMATION SEARCH POINTS INSIDE

To Tasha, my beloved and exceptional wife, with whom I made the 'big move' and without whom this journey would have been ten times harder and far less worthwhile.

CONTENTS

*The prudent man obtains knowledge, and the ear of a wise
man seeks it out. – Proverbs 18:15*

*"Whatever the mind of man can conceive and believe, it can
achieve." – Napoleon Hill*

• HEREIN IS KNOWLEDGE •

D erville is a native of Montego Bay – the tourism capital of the beautiful Caribbean Island of Jamaica. Born on the 24th of November 1981 to working-class parents, he is the last of four children.

His father – Clifford Lowe, is a Carpenter who never ceased his labor and a most skillful artisan. His mother – Jewette Lowe is a Cook, Domestic Worker, Homemaker, Bee Farmer, et al, who never sat still and did whatever her hands found to do in order to take care of her family and make ends meet.

Growing up in the tight-knit community of Glendevon in a working-class family on the fringes of poverty, he learned the value and importance of hard work, faith in God, respect, good behavior and education. Principles from which he never departed and which gave him the inner drive to push boundaries, explore possibilities, try new things, be determined and focused and pursue the extraordinary.

Having a strong foundation laid for his early education, he attended the Glendevon Primary and Junior High School *(formerly Glendevon All Age School)* located in his community. In 1994, he was successful in his exit exams at the elementary level and was subsequently awarded a place at Cornwall College – one of Jamaica's foremost 'traditional' high schools for boys.

Being unsuccessful in securing the required subjects in his high school exit examinations in 1999, disappointment set in, but he did not give up.

It was a decisive moment – either give up in despair or keep trying. The latter was the prudent option and with his mother's encouragement, he later had the opportunity to attend the Harrison Memorial High School – A Seventh-day Adventist-operated school in Montego Bay. Here, things took a turn for the best and under the exemplary tutelage of his teachers, he successfully completed eight subjects at the secondary level in the sciences and arts. This success qualified him to be matriculated at the Northern Caribbean University in Manchester, Jamaica in 2002.

Attending Northern Caribbean University (NCU) was a dream come true and turned out to be a most fulfilling and rewarding experience. While at NCU, he served as Resident Advisor, Treasurer of the Excelsior Club (a club for male dorm residents) and was a Bass/Baritone in the university's chamber ensemble. It was also here that he had his foray into entrepreneurship, after being selected a top awardee in the Young Entrepreneurs Competition run by the then Churches (now First Heritage) Cooperative Credit Union. It was exciting times!

In 2008, he earned his Bachelor of Science Degree in Information Science with a Minor in Business, which was a huge milestone. That same year he became a Global Korea Scholar after submitting an application for, and subsequently being awarded a

Korean Government Scholarship to pursue graduate studies in the Republic of Korea.

Derville lived in South Korea for three years (2008 to 2011), where he studied the Korean Language at Silla University in Busan for one year. Upon completion of the intensive, year-long language course, he transferred to Woosuk University in Jeonju. Here he completed his MBA in International Business after successfully defending his research thesis, which was a study of the economic relationship between Jamaica and the Republic of Korea.

An Author, Writer & Editor, Linguist, Content Creator, Entrepreneur and internationally experienced Administrative Professional, he has worked for the Jamaican, South Korean and Canadian governments in various administrative roles. He speaks four languages, namely, English, Korean, Spanish and French and is a Published Author and Socio-political Writer with numerous topical articles published in Jamaica's major newspapers – The Gleaner and The Observer.

He migrated to Canada with his wife in 2017 – a risky but life-changing decision. God provided a way and provided unexpected, but much needed help along the way. He and his wife settled in Kelowna, a city situated on the Okanagan Lake in the Southern

Interior and the seventh largest in the Province of British Columbia.

His experience in Canada included delivering employment-related services through the Employment Program of British Columbia (EPBC) to the residents of Kelowna and the City of Mission. His experience has given him first-hand knowledge and invaluable insight which are penned in this book.

It is the author's hope that this book will help each immigrant who reads it, to have a smooth, stress-free transition and settlement into their new home and that all their dreams, expectations and ambitions in Canada become a reality.

This guide was prepared with the sole intention of providing information that has proven to be most overlooked by prospective Canadian Immigrants. Having experienced how arduous the process can be and how challenging it is to find proper guidance on this matter, the author has compiled essential information in this simple guide to make preparation for moving to Canada a less stressful undertaking.

Overlooking simple steps in preparing to migrate, as well as key details in preparing an application package can be frustrating, time consuming and result in mental fatigue and financial loss. This simple guide was put together with the hope that aspiring immigrants will take a few moments to read it and find useful the experience, facts, tips, and advice which the author presents herein. This information is to give you a push forward that you most likely didn't have before reading this guide.

One of the many lessons I have learnt in writing this book is that - when God gives you inspiration, run with it! Writing this book has been nothing short of an out-of-body experience for me. It was written as a response to the needs and plethora of questions that prospective immigrants have and the many issues new immigrants face.

I started taking writing seriously in 2013 and fell in love with it. I neither thought I would be a writer nor ever dreamt of becoming one; it was beyond me. However, God blessed my little brain with thoughts, insight and ideas and I often have full-fledged conversations with myself (not that I'm crazy; it just helps me keep my ideas flowing).

Since moving to Canada in 2017, I have learned a lot and gained a wealth of knowledge and wisdom. A number of persons were instrumental in this growth, namely, Cary B., Eva K. and Larry A., to name a few! These awesome people from the Maximus Canada Employment Services team taught me a lot and for that I am eternally grateful.

Over the course of the two years I've lived in Canada, I came to the realization that many immigrants, including myself, were facing a plethora of challenges with settling. This was especially evident when it came to finding suitable and sustainable employment. Job searching in a new labor market comes with its fair share of challenges. New immigrants, not having the knowledge or experience, often find it difficult to adjust.

As destiny would have it, I was on LinkedIn one day while at the office and decided to give a brief response to the lamentation of one of my few connections. He was an immigrant who was having a hard time finding suitable employment commensurate with his skills and training. After reading his post, I felt compelled to shed some light on how persons could better prepare for immigrating to Canada and how to search for work when they arrive.

As I typed my response, I recognized it was getting a bit lengthy so, as I usually do, I copied and pasted it into Microsoft Word with the intention of responding to said LinkedIn post. While typing what I thought would have been a simple response to someone's concerns about Canada's labor market, I realized I wasn't slowing down to bring an end to my response. I was typing continuously and the words kept flowing from brain to paper.

Minutes turned to hours, hours to days and days to weeks. After a few weeks of emptying my knowledge coupled with my personal experience into the word processor, I finally stopped typing. I leaned back in my chair and said to myself – wow! This book was happening in real time and I did not see it coming. This is what you call destiny.

What was intended to be a simple response to a LinkedIn post, transformed into a full-fledged book! Up to this point I only had a few articles published in Jamaica's major newspapers – The Gleaner and The Observer. This was new territory for me but it felt really good that I was doing it. It was a new frontier; a new accomplishment; even though I had no idea what to do next.

Having developed the habit of taking my concerns, plans, dreams and goals to God, I prayed about it, asking Him for direction. I then got to searching the internet and started scouting publishers, reading reviews and researching how to publish a book. After a couple of days of searching and getting a basic understanding of publishing ins and outs, I decided to contact Balboa Press (A division of Hay House) in the United States. They appeared to be publishers I could work with to get my book to the world – and they were.

This was an absolute leap of faith because I knew nothing about this company, with the exception of the reviews I read online.

Following a few telephone conversations and a thread of emails with a publishing consultant, I felt comfortable enough to move forward and subsequently signed a publishing contract. My response to a LinkedIn post, turned book, became my first book project and maiden voyage into the world of authorship.

Three months from the day I started writing this book, it was finally ready for printing and distribution. This was surreal, jaw-dropping and a real tearjerker for me – ha-ha. I never planned it and literally never saw it coming. Simply put – when God gives you inspiration – RUN WITH IT.

The first edition of *"Immigrating to Canada? Prepare for Change"* was published on September 3, 2019.

This book was revised and improved to give more depth and scope to the subject of immigrating to Canada. The revision is done with the intent to provide more clarity and with the hope that prospective immigrants will find the help and guidance they need. The author hopes that the knowledge shared herein will help each one with planning, preparation and transition as they make the 'big move' to Canada.

Whatever the purpose is for your move to Canada, this book is the resource that you need to help you prepare yourself and your family. It is written to provide insight and decrease, or entirely remove the hassle and frustration that usually comes with making such a risky and life-changing decision.

The first publication received very good reviews, but this newly revised and redesigned edition is more comprehensive and promises to be even more valuable to the reader.

Readers the world over have given this book the highest ratings and reviews. Here are a few:

"This is a must read! If you are planning to Migrate to Canada, this book is just what you are looking for!" – Dr. Ana Figueroa, El Salvador

"Migrating to Canada? Must Read!! Amazing read for anyone who is looking to migrate to Canada." – Paulette Grant, USA

"A Must Read! An honest and unfiltered take on the Canadian immigration experience." – Tracy-Ann Curate-Phillips, Jamaica

"The 'I wish someone told me this' Guide. Really clearly written. The information is very useful and provides a lot of clarity on misconceptions." – Amazon Customer, USA

"A Must Read. Exceptional knowledge earned from reading this book." – Kerry-Ann Hicks, USA

"The reader-friendly immigrant bible. This book was an informative read. It captures the salient points that every new immigrant should be aware of." – Kayon Lightbody, Canada

My deepest desire is that these ratings and reviews will find factual affirmation among those who read this new and improved edition. I am grateful for this opportunity to share my experience and knowledge and am confident that someone will be helped through their reading of what is herein written.

Sincerely,

CHAPTER ONE
Making the Big Decision
-

My wife and I were home on a warm evening in April 2017 when she and I had a sit-down to discuss our future. We discussed the things we would like to accomplish in the medium to long-term, as well as how best we could help out our parents financially as they got older.

We were living apart at the time as a result of our jobs. She was working in Montego Bay and I in Kingston, Jamaica. We looked at our situation and both agreed that we needed a change, especially since the distance started taking a toll on our young marriage. The 'magnifying glass' came out and after some introspection and analysis, we came to the conclusion that migrating would be a good thing for us to do.

My wife had previously worked in the United States of America for a while – Boston, Massachusetts to be exact – and did not desire to return there to work and settle. I was in complete agreement since I was not fond of going to the United States to work either. With that consensus in mind, we proceeded to explore the option of immigrating to Canada.

After doing some basic research online and speaking with some friends who were already living in 'the land of Maple Leaf', we decided it was a good option to take a stab at – and so we did.

My wife had a strong desire to pursue further studies; hence, after some checking, we chose the study route. After searching for a suitable program of study for her, we settled on Okanagan College (OC) in Kelowna, British Columbia. Not only did this college offer her preferred program of study, but it was a Designated Learning Institution (DLI) and was situated in one of the warmest parts of Canada – or so we were told. In Canada, warmth is relative. Just ensure you get the appropriate clothing and prepare yourself for winter. Winters in Canada are no joke.

We would later find out that Kelowna's 'warmth' was not as advertised. In fact, the City of Abbotsford (and the Vancouver Metro Area by extension) in the Lower Mainland, as well as Vancouver Island, experiences shorter and less harsh winter seasons and even gets less snow fall than Kelowna does. The lesson – always take what you hear with a grain of salt. This lesson was served cold and well learned.

My wife opted to apply for the two-year Diploma program in Criminal Justice at Okanagan College, which made sense since she was a practicing Social Worker in Jamaica. A few weeks later she received an offer of admission, which was the single most important piece of the puzzle in applying to the Canadian High Commission for a student visa.

Another very important piece of the puzzle needed to apply for a study visa was proof of available funds. This is usually in the form of a recent bank statement. This was to prove that we were capable of covering tuition fees, travel and living expenses for at least one year after arriving in Canada.

Sourcing the necessary funds initially seemed daunting as we needed to provide proof that we had at least twenty-five thousand Canadian dollars (CAN$25,000) or approximately JM$2.5 million, which, as you may have guessed, we did not have stashed away anywhere.

What did we do? First, we sold our cars. We had two cars at the time since we lived and worked in different cities. My wife was a Social Worker with the Western Regional Health Authority in Montego

Bay and I was a Researcher with the Embassy of the Republic of Korea, Kingston.

My car was being financed and had a lien against it; therefore, I had an obligation to pay off what I owed to the bank before it was signed over to a new owner. Thankfully I got an offer shortly after putting my car on the market. This was indeed a blessing. After selling it, I cleared my arrears and was left with a decent balance which went directly into funding our big move. We also sold our appliances (stove and refrigerator) and finally, to make up the deficit, we applied for a personal loan from a preferred financial institution. It all worked out in the end. We had just enough to provide the proof of funds that we needed for our visa application.

We prepared all the other relevant documentation and set an appointment at the Visa Application Center (VAC). This is where all visa applications to travel to Canada are submitted. The VAC provided the necessary assistance to complete and submit the official visa application package and it is here that we also provided our biometrics.

I will pause here to share some vital bits of information that future applicants need to know:

1. The Canadian High Commission does not accept visa applications directly. The Government of

Canada has contracted Visa Application Centers globally, to provide visa application support and biometrics services to applicants for Canadian visas and other immigration services.

2. It is important that you know the services VACs offer. For a small fee, they assist applicants with completing applications; securely transmit passport and decision documents to the Canadian High Commission for processing. They may also provide access to a computer to complete online applications; provide photograph and copy services; and help set up courier services to return relevant documents to applicants.

3. Not all VACs provide comprehensive services, hence it is important that applicants contact the nearest VAC to make specific inquiries. The location, contact information, services provided and general instructions can be found online at the following website:

   https://www.vfsglobal.ca/Canada/

4. The Canadian Government DOES NOT use agents to recruit applicants, therefore, shun the very appearance of that well-dressed "agent" who shows up at your home, office or on the street offering Canadian immigration services.

Individuals have been scammed by imposters in the past. Be warned and be vigilant.

5. In preparation for your big move to Canada - READ, READ, READ - please. Check everything for yourself and be in the know. I can't stress the importance of this enough. Even if you chose to use the services of a consultant, it never hurts to check and know the facts for yourself. It is not only safer and empowering to have that first-hand knowledge, but it significantly decreases the chances of you making a mistake, while it increases your overall preparedness and success. Furthermore, you decrease the chances of being bamboozled or mislead. So, before you get the ball rolling, be informed.

A few important things to research are:

- Apartment types, location, availability and rental costs
- Cost of child care (if applicable)
- School District (if applicable)
- Occupations in demand
- Potential job openings and salary ranges
- Public Transit System
- Weather conditions and what you need based on the season in which you are traveling

Further information on immigrating to Canada and immigration rules and regulations can be found on the following website:

https://www.canada.ca/en/services/immigration-citizenship.html

Approximately five weeks after my wife submitted her application, her study visa was issued. For me, that was pretty quick. With that, I was then eligible to apply for an Open Work Permit as I was now classified as the spouse of an international student. An Open Work Permit allows the holder to work for any employer in Canada, with the exception of regulated occupations and those specified as prohibited on the work permit.

Do you need a work permit? *To find out more, please visit the following website:*

https://www.canada.ca/en/immigration-refugees-citizenship/services/work-canada/permit/temporary/need-work-permit-work.html

Following the same procedure my wife used, I prepared my application package for a work visa and open work permit. I gathered the required documents and set up an appointment at the VAC, where I received the necessary assistance to submit my application package. My application was processed and within six weeks my work visa was approved.

Being granted the appropriate visas was only permission for us to travel to Canada, but not the actual study or work permits. The permits to study and work in Canada are separate documents. The actual permits were issued by Canadian Immigration/Border Services at the first international airport where we landed in Canada – **please take note of this**.

Starting a new life in Canada is a huge step and milestone in your life. It is probably one of the biggest changes you will ever make. For most immigrants it is the only such move they will make for the rest of their lives. You are going to do this only once, so it behooves you to do it right.

Further information to help you in your preparation for this life-changing move and to make your transition easier, is available at the following website:

https://www.canada.ca/en/immigration-refugees-citizenship/services/new-immigrants/new-life-canada.html

Here's a link to a video that gives an overview of what you need to know and do ***before*** immigrating to Canada:

https://www.canada.ca/en/immigration-refugees-citizenship/news/video/before-you-arrive-canada.html

Here's a link to a video that gives you information on things you need to know and do ***within the first two weeks*** of arrival in Canada:

https://www.canada.ca/en/immigration-refugees-citizenship/news/video/your-first-two-weeks-canada.html

Point to note:

Spouses of international students are eligible to apply for an open work permit.

*You will not receive a work or study permit prior to your arrival in Canada. Work Permits are issued by the Canada Border Services Agency at the first international airport of disembarkation in Canada. **DO NOT leave the airport without the relevant permit.***

CHAPTER TWO

Change Starts Pre-departure

-

Life started changing long before we packed up and left home. We had to resign our jobs which were pretty decent by Jamaican standards – I was Researcher at the Korean Embassy, Kingston and my wife a Social Worker with the Ministry of Health working with people living with HIV/AIDS. We had to sell what could be sold and get to packing what we could carry in order to decrease the expenses once we moved. It was a lot of work, but Canada beckoned.

God, knowing our plans even before we did, would have seen our future and set up some help for us before we even knew it. One warm Kingston evening, my neighbor – Mr. Wood and I got to talking across the fence and I decided to share with him that my wife and I were moving to Canada.

He was pleasantly surprised and shared with me that he had a long-time friend living there and asked where in Canada I was going. I told him I was heading to Kelowna in British Columbia; a name that sounded familiar to him. As it turned out, that is where his friends were living. He happily made the connection and they agreed to receive us when we arrive. Hooked up from heaven I call it.

Having someone receive you when you first arrive in Canada is a huge advantage as it makes settling easier, relieves the stress of finding a place immediately, saves you money and you have someone who knows the territory to guide and assist you. This really helped to make the transition smoother and to get important things done, such as opening a bank account; getting your Social Insurance Number (SIN) and finding resources for apartment hunting, etc.

It is also a tremendous help to have somewhere to stay for your first few days or weeks as you search for a suitable apartment to rent. This also significantly minimize or at best, remove expenses related to accommodation at a hotel, hostel or motel. So, before you travel, it is a good thing to check in with family or friends to see if they know someone living in the city you are moving to and make that connection for you. Trust me, it helps a great deal.

If you have not made any arrangements for someone to receive you and your family when you arrive in Canada, it is important that you secure short-term accommodation before you arrive. Take the time to search for and reserve a room at a hotel, motel or hostel in a central location in your destination city. Take care in where you choose and ensure that you can make reservations and make payment through a secure and official online platform. Once your reservation is made and you receive confirmation, print out the confirmation and take it with you when you travel. This piece of documentation is very important.

Speaking of documentation – before you do anything else, please remember to gather ALL your important documents. First and foremost is your Passport. Then, ensure you have the letter you received from the Canadian Embassy or Consulate in your country – ***do not forget it***. This letter is to be presented to the Border Services Officer at the airport when you arrive for verification.

Other documents you will need include – national IDs (e.g. driver's license), your birth certificate, academic certificate(s) or degree(s), health record, marriage certificate, language certificate(s) and any other relevant personal documents.

Place them in a water-tight enclosure and pack them safely into your carry-on luggage. This will ensure safekeeping and allow you to have quick access to them on the go.

Communication is one of the most important things to pay attention to when moving to a new country. Canada is no different. Canada has two official languages, namely, English and French; with Quebec being the only majority French-speaking Province in the country. However, many French-speakers live and work in other Provinces across Canada. Many companies also require their employees to have bilingual proficiency in the two official languages, especially federal jobs such as those in immigration, social services and other government services.

If you are not originally from an English or French-speaking country or you are not fluent in either language, it is recommended that you find a language class and start learning before you travel to Canada, if possible. French is especially necessary if you are planning on settling in Quebec.

If you are unable to access language classes prior to your arrival in Canada, do not worry. There are many institutions and service centers for immigrants where you may be able to access classes for English and/or French.

Here is an **informational video** to give you some guidance as to what you need to know **prior to your arrival** in Canada. Take the time to watch it. The ten minutes you spend here will be of great help.

https://www.canada.ca/en/immigration-refugees-citizenship/news/video/before-you-arrive-canada.html

CHAPTER **THREE**
Arrival in Canada

-

When we arrived at the Kelowna International Airport on August 17, 2017, Mrs. Haughton, a petit Jamaican lady, greeted us sweetly and invited us to pack our luggage into her car. Her little son, Pish, seemed quite excited to meet the new Jamaican strangers and also helped us get our luggage safely stowed away. The first stop on our way to her home was Boston Pizza – our first introduction to the City of Kelowna – the place we would call home for the foreseeable future.

When we met the other members of her family, they also welcomed us just as sweetly and made us feel at home. It was a nice way to start life in Canada. We could not ask for a better welcome. We were in Canada and because we had help, the apprehension that came with being newbies was pretty much off our shoulders. Mrs. Haughton offered to be our personal chauffeur and took us to open our new bank accounts at TD Bank and also to Service

Canada where we got our Social Insurance Number (SIN).

It was early Autumn so it was just the right temperature and very beautiful outside, but Winter was not far away and more challenges were ahead. We were extremely grateful to God for hooking us up with the Haughton's. We were soon introduced to Leon – another Jamaican, who picked us up one day and brought us to Fred – an Iranian car dealer. Fred also welcomed us warmly and gave us the best deal he could find, given the small budget we had to purchase a car.

The pickings were slim, of course, but we settled on a 2000 Acura TX with two hundred and fifty thousand (250,000) miles on the odometer (wow!), for which we paid two thousand five hundred dollars ($2500). Despite the high mileage, the car was in pretty decent condition and served us well.

When moving to a new country, it is very helpful to have someone receive you when you arrive. This allows for an easier transition and minimizes the challenges which come with settling. New immigrants without this help usually find it a lot more stressful, especially to move around to get the essentials in place at the beginning. If it were not for this help, we would have been forced to start spending immediately on motel or hostel accommodation, transportation and meals, which would have depleted our inelastic financial resources. Thank God for the help He sent.

Here is an **informational video** to give you some guidance as to what to do during the first two weeks **after you arrive** in Canada. Take the time to watch it. The ten minutes you spend here will be of great help.

https://www.canada.ca/en/immigration-refugees-citizenship/news/video/your-first-two-weeks-canada.html

Points to note:

A bank account and your Social Security Number (SIN) are immediate must haves. You are encouraged to get these two things as soon as you get settled.

Once you land in Canada, expenses immediately start and there is no break, no holiday, no time to think and the law stipulates that you are considered a 'resident' for tax purposes.

CHAPTER **FOUR**
How to Find Housing

-

After settling in for a couple of days and getting acclimatized, we started the relentless and exhausting quest for an apartment. Nothing prepared us for the laborious experience which consisted of searching for available units online; making phone calls to potential landlords; sending emails and setting up appointments for viewing. Searching for an apartment is hard, but finding the ideal apartment is even harder. Frankly speaking, it was time consuming and sometimes frustrating.

The key to apartment hunting is to start early in the morning, check monthly rates, check availability date and find out if utilities are included, if any. Finding a unit with utilities included in the monthly rent is ideal but less available due to market demand.

To help you narrow your search and determine the most suitable place to rent an apartment, use google maps to determine the distance from your potential residence to your workplace or school. Get information regarding public transit services if you don't plan on buying a car immediately. Then, set up appointments with prospective landlords and pack as many viewings in a day as best as you possibly can.

I recommend renting a basement suite rather than an apartment in a strata-type complex, if possible. This decision really comes down to your personal preference, convenience, comfort and of course, availability.

The home-owner landlords tend to be more personable and have more flexibility than the strata/property management companies which tend to be more rigid and inflexible. If you are fortunate enough to get a basement suite, your monthly rent may include utilities such as electricity/hydro, internet and water. If not, you may be able to negotiate having utilities included for a little higher rental charge.

You may also be able to rent a unit on a month-to-month basis, which will allow you the flexibility to relocate whenever you choose, since you will not be locked into a one-year contract. This type of arrangement also works in the interest of the landlords, since it affords them the opportunity to determine if you are the right tenant for them.

In your search for a place to call home, you will eventually find a potential winner. When you do, NEVER EVER make an electronic transfer or down payment on an apartment before viewing the space and meeting the potential landlord *in person*. Scammers abound and often pose as legitimate landlords on websites such as craigslist, so exercise caution when searching online.

A rule of thumb when searching for a place to live is - *if the photos and amenities you see being advertised online look too good to be true, then assume it is not true*. Do not be tricked by fancy or over-the-top offerings being advertised online. Be vigilant and ensure the listings are legitimate and available before you make any arrangements to view or pay a deposit.

Legitimate landlords will have real addresses and be available to meet you and give you a walk through in person. Therefore, if the person on the other end of the email thread or phone call is in Paris or Mexico on vacation, delete their contact information immediately and keep it moving.

A key point to bear in mind when searching for an apartment is that they usually become available to be rented to new tenants on the 1st or 15th of each month, so timing is crucial.

If you are planning to move-in at the beginning of the ensuing month, I recommend you conduct your search during the last two weeks of the current month. For example – if you want a move-in ready apartment for September 1, you should book viewings between August 15 and 30. If the desired move-in date is September 15, set viewing appointments between August 30 and September 14.

Otherwise, if you find a place you like and you want it to be held for you, you may have to pay for the extra days, which will only dig into your finances. This can be avoided if you search at the right time or your potential landlord is very nice and agrees you can move in early without incurring extra charges. If the latter happens, good for you; just be grateful and enjoy your new home.

Most expenses, including your rent, will be paid online by you or via a pre-authorized withdrawal (the most frequently used method) from your Canadian bank account. This is one of the main reasons you should open a new bank account as soon as you arrive in Canada.

Furnishing Your Apartment

Rental units are usually available either furnished or unfurnished. If you do not want, or are unable to find a furnished apartment, don't worry about furnishing too much as there are several options to source what you will need to make your new place homey. New furniture is quite expensive so I strongly encourage purchasing used furniture that is in good condition, such as - sofas, side tables, bar stools, dining sets and bed bases.

There are many thrift stores and second-hand retailers such as Value Village, where you can buy cheap, used furniture in good condition. Facebook Marketplace is also another good source to search for such items. It is super active and usually has great deals on furniture being sold directly by the owners.

Even if the furniture has a few scratches and look a bit worn, you can restore them by yourself. All you need to do is drop by Walmart or Home Depot and grab sand paper and a couple cans of spray paint and just make it a fun DIY project that you and your family can enjoy together.

That is what we did and it was fun; plus, we were very happy with the outcome. Simply join one or more local Facebook buy/sell groups to get access to some great deals (**Hint***: it is also a good place to advertise and sell things that you will eventually want to get rid of in the future*).

The one thing that I am absolutely sure you will need is a good night's rest. Therefore, the only thing I would suggest you purchase new are mattresses and I think you know why. The exception of course, is if you check the merchandise and you are very comfortable with the condition of a used one (like we initially did), then feel free to purchase it.

Some mattresses are returned to stores by the first buyer after being purchased and briefly used. Depending on where you are looking, you may find used mattresses for resale at a discounted price, which have been professionally cleaned and restored to factory-like condition. If you find such a deal, take it. You should plan to spend about two hundred and fifty dollars ($250) – give or take – which is a good ballpark figure for a new eight-inch, queen-sized mattress at Walmart or similar retailers. The amount you spend on a mattress really comes down to size, type, styling, brand and where you buy it.

For further information on apartment rental in Canada, please visit the following websites:

https://www.cmhc-schl.gc.ca/en/housing-observer-online/2018-housing-observer/national-vacancy-rate-falls-below-average-last-10-years

https://www.chf.bc.ca/2018-canadian-rental-housing-index-shows-renters-in-a-crisis-level-of-spending/

https://globalnews.ca/news/4194216/provinces-cities-canada-highest-lowest-rent/

Points to note:

When searching for an apartment or suite to rent, bear in mind that they usually become available to be rented to new tenants on the 1st or 15th of each month, so timing is critical.

*ALWAYS view a potential apartment or suite **in person**, with the landlord present, before making any deposit payments or signing a contract.*

NEVER do viewings and make payments virtually, except in a situation where someone you know is viewing on your behalf.

CHAPTER **FIVE**

Living Expenses

-

The Cost of Living in Canada

The cost of living in Canada varies from city to city; province to province and is influenced by various factors. Someone once told me that when it comes to housing market, one major factor to consider is – location, location, location. This, I have proven to be factual.

Many immigrants like the idea of living in populous urban areas and make plans to do so without carefully considering the high expenses associated with living in these urban centers. For instance – Toronto, the financial capital of Canada, is a hot spot and magnet for immigrants. The City of Toronto reportedly has the highest rental cost; with over twenty percent (20%) of people spending fifty percent (50%) or more of their income on rent alone.

According to a rental market survey conducted in 2019, people who desire to live in Vancouver needed to be earning at least twenty-six dollars ($26) per hour (that is twice the minimum wage), in order to afford renting a one (1) bedroom apartment there. The survey also pointed out that people earning the minimum wage would need to work a whopping eighty-four (84) hours per week in order to afford renting a one (1) bedroom apartment in Vancouver while having to take care of other living expenses.

I suggest you avoid large urban areas like Toronto and Vancouver if you can, as the living expenses will be very high and arduous. This is important for persons or families that are just starting out, especially if you are single or have children. What I recommend you do instead, is start at a place where the cost of living is more affordable. If you so desire, you can relocate to a larger city in the future when you are more established, have a financial base, more knowledgeable of and prepared for the demands and financial requirements of 'the big city life'.

Spending on average thirty percent (30%) of your income on your rent is generally considered the affordability threshold in Canada. Nevertheless, more than forty percent (40%) of renters are said to exceed this threshold. Before you come to Canada, I strongly advise that you research the rental rates in your destination city. This will significantly boost your preparedness for your impending living expenses. Homelessness in Canada is real and immigrants are not immune to it, so please ***plan well***. That is an experience that you really want to avoid at all cost.

To get an idea of what the cost of living in Canada looks like, please visit the following websites:

🔍🌐 https://www.internations.org/go/moving-to-canada/living/the-cost-of-living-in-canada

🔍🌐 https://www.immigrationworld.com/canada/cost-of-living-in-canada/

General Expenses

There is really no option to purchasing the things you need for daily living, especially food; with the exception of planting a spring garden if you have the space. It may seem like a given, but if you are from a tropical country or a place where you usually plant fruits, vegetables and herbs in your home garden or they grow in the wild, this will make more sense to you.

The key is to be prudent in your shopping. Do not just shop; make sure you search for deals and compare prices.

Many retailers in Canada will price match, so shopping around and comparing prices will save you money.

If your monthly rental does not include utilities, you can get a basic internet/cable/home phone package from one of the many service providers. Owing to the competitive nature of Canada's telecommunications market, your negotiation skills may come in handy as it may result in lowering your monthly payments for services. Most internet/cable contracts are for a two-year period with certain terms and conditions attached, so make sure you know what you are signing to before entering into a contract. READ THE FINE PRINT.

Getting a mobile phone in Canada has become fairly easy as telecommunication companies have relaxed the requirements for new immigrants to sign up for services. Nevertheless, you may use your current mobile device in Canada as long as it is unlocked. If your phone is compatible, all you will need to do is purchase a new SIM card or you can opt to get a new phone on a fixed plan with data, international minutes, etc.

Bear in mind that Canada is known to have one of the highest costs for mobile services globally.

As it pertains to electricity (or hydro), what you pay per billing period is really based on your usage. Your hydro bill however, can increase significantly during the winter months due to heating. One way to lower your energy bill during winter, is to get a small portable space heater instead of using central heating. Also make sure your apartment is as air-tight as possible.

Of course, larger apartments will require more energy since they take longer to warm up, so in this case, size matter. You can also opt to wear warmer clothing inside and use less heating. NEVER use other household appliances such as a clothing iron or oven to warm up your apartment. You really don't want to be the person to set a house or apartment complex on fire. When using portable heaters, take all the necessary precautions to avoid a fire and follow the usage instructions carefully. A wise person once said – prevention is better than cure.

Points to note:

If you rent a strata-type apartment, you may incur additional costs for parking, laundry services and home insurance.

You should avoid living in big cities as the cost of living will be much higher than living on the outskirts or in a smaller city or nearby town.

CHAPTER SIX

Migrating to Work?
Know the demands in the Canadian Labor Market

-

People primarily move to Canada for one of two reasons – either to study or to work. In this chapter, we will discuss the latter.

It is very important for you to know the career path, occupation or profession that you would like to pursue once you settle in Canada. Why? There are various layers to the Canadian labor market that immigrants need to peel away in order to have a clear picture of the opportunities available to them. The Federal and Provincial Governments, based on statistics collected and labor demand trends, makes the determination as to what sectors of the labor market will need people over a projected number of years.

Each province has varying levels of demand for each occupation. The demand for Teachers and Truck

Drivers in British Columbia for example, is not the same as in Saskatchewan. Each city within a province also has varying levels of demand for each occupation or profession. For instance, in British Columbia, the demand for administrative workers is higher in Vancouver than in Abbotsford; but demand for Farm Workers is higher in Abbotsford than in Vancouver.

Most prospective immigrants are often told or see advertisements online that there are 'many jobs in Canada' for the taking and that 'Canada needs people'. This misinformation usually entices wary prospects and triggers excitement rather than careful consideration. Not that I intend to crush anyone's dreams but this excitement is unfortunately misplaced and the notion is false.

Many jobs may be available in Canada but as the saying goes, the devil is in the details. I just want to warn aspiring immigrants here, to pay close attention to the details when considering immigrating to Canada for work. While there is some truth to the notion that there are many jobs available across Canada, it is usually at the city level that we find people searching for work and it is here that many immigrants face the harsh realities of the job search process and labor market mechanisms.
Migrating to Canada for work takes a lot of planning and patience. The outcome of your job search is

dependent on several factors including – your location, what field you are in, the type of jobs in demand, your training and experience, and what jobs are available at the time of your search. It is a process that can easily become frustrating if you do not have the right information on the labor market in your destination city prior to arrival.

Chances are, you may have heard statements like – 'all you need to have in order to get a job in Canada is a degree' – this is simply not the truth. As a matter of fact, it could not be farther from the truth. Although you may have a college degree, you may not be qualified for the 'ideal' or more lucrative employment opportunities for various reasons. These reasons include – not having Canadian work experience or lacking the required Canadian certification or licensing, which is mandatory for regulated occupations. Many employers prefer hiring immigrants who have some experience working in Canada; even if for only three months, it counts.

Many employment opportunities in Canada do not necessarily require a degree, but rather, specific hard skills and hands-on capabilities which will enable you to carry out the assigned tasks.

Jobs in areas such as sales, retail, fast food, hospitality or customer service, do not require persons to have degrees. Many employers in the aforementioned sectors also provide on-the-job, paid training to new employees.

Truth be told, only a handful of immigrants will land the ideal job shortly after they arrive in Canada. As was mentioned earlier, expenses will be upon you as soon as you land, so it is crucial to get to work asap in order to prevent depletion of your funds. Realistically speaking, you will probably have to start with a minimum wage job and juggle multiple jobs in order to comfortably cover your living expenses and hopefully have some left over for saving, which will no doubt come in handy.

In your job search, you may find that you will have little or no choice but to accept an available job that will get you working and cover your necessary expenses. You may also need to get additional training in order to qualify for your preferred job or the more lucrative employment opportunities. Of utmost importance is that you DO YOUR OWN RESEARCH.

You will give yourself an advantage if you know the labor market demands and the qualifications which are required across industries, especially in your destination city, before you arrive. This knowledge will give you a more realistic outlook and make your job search far less stressful.

I cannot place enough emphasis on how important it is to know the demands of the labor market before you make this big move. It is imperative that you take the time to know what is happening in your destination city, so that when you arrive with your 'big degree', years of experience and high expectations, you are not disappointed when all you can get is a job at McDonalds, Seven Eleven or Walmart.

You will not know it all, but at the least, you will be informed and better prepared to meet the challenges ahead.

Do not drive through the fog of immigration with one headlight on. It always pays to be in the know.

The Job Bank is an excellent resource to search for jobs by demand, popularity, province, category and employer. You can get started here:

 https://www.jobbank.gc.ca/browsejobs

Point to note:

Much attention needs to be given to your current occupation to see if it will soon be replaced by technology. This is an important factor in determining whether you will find a job faster, require additional training or even get a career change. Don't forget that you are competing with Canadians as well as a plethora of other immigrants who are also seeking jobs.

CHAPTER **SEVEN**

Know your National Occupational Classification (NOC) Code

-

All occupations or professions in Canada are classified using a National Occupational Classification (NOC) Code. You are encouraged check and know the NOC under which your occupation falls. This will help you to narrow your job search in Canada and better equip you to find necessary information on the skills and qualifications required in specific fields. Once you ascertain your NOC, you can use it to pinpoint the specific employment opportunities in your field; view job descriptions, labor market trends, salary ranges and whether your primary occupation is regulated or unregulated.

Regulated occupations in Canada require a specific certification or license from the relevant government body or registered regulatory agency.

Once you have successfully completed the requisite training and examinations and received your license or certification, this will permit you to engage in specialized jobs in specific industries which are regulated by the Canadian Government. This knowledge is invaluable as it limits the frustration when doing a job search.

The NOC consists 4 digits – each digit having a specific meaning which contextually designates what is required for each job category. Generally speaking, immigrants are usually classified as "skilled workers", hence most occupations undertaken by immigrants commonly fall under NOC codes designated by skill type 'o' (managerial); skill levels A (professional) and B (technical and trade jobs).

Many Canadian employers also use the NOC code to find suitable employees in the labor market who have specific training and experience. This helps them to pinpoint the most suitable candidates, while saving them time and avoiding unnecessary and generalized recruitment.

Your NOC is also a key piece of information that you will need to know when you are completing the work history section of your express entry profile when you are applying for permanent residence.

To check the category, code and skill type of your occupation, please visit the following website:

 https://www.canada.ca/en/immigration-refugees-citizenship/services/immigrate-canada/express-entry/eligibility/find-national-occupation-code.html#noc

Point to note:

Knowing your NOC code and where to find it will also come in very handy when the time comes for you to prepare your application for permanent residence (PR). The PR application will require you to supply all the NOC codes for your past and current employment, whether inside or outside of Canada.

CHAPTER **EIGHT**
Job Searching in Canada
-

Job searching in Canada is probably the one thing for which most immigrants are ill-prepared. The first thing you need to understand is that you are coming in with zero Canadian work experience and many employers prefer hiring persons who have this.

That said, the vast majority of immigrants will have no choice but to accept a job that is way below their qualification and experience just to get the ball rolling, while they continue searching for more suitable employment opportunities. Only a handful of new immigrants will land the ideal job shortly after they arrive.

As I mentioned earlier, your expenses become due as soon as you land so it is important to get to work asap. Yes, it will probably mean you have to work for the minimum wage or a little above and even do multiple jobs in order to comfortably cover your expenses, but it is absolutely important that you get to work.

This is where patience and perseverance will be needed most; especially for those who are coming out of a higher end job in their home country. For students, it is even more difficult as fees and bills pile up easily. The law dictates that immigrants with a student visa can only work for twenty (20) hours per week and students who exceed this stipulation put themselves at risk of deportation.

Truth is, both immigrants and Canadians share the common struggle to find sustainable employment, not to mention many of the indigenous people (this has to be discussed in another book). Unfortunately, the job market and finding jobs are not as straightforward as we would like.

Knowing the type of occupation that you want to undertake or the industry you wish to work in, is also important in your preparation. This can save you a lot of time, money and frustration, as you will, through your search, be able to narrow down where and how many potential jobs are available and whether your skills are in demand in your destination province or city.

You will also be able to gauge the requirements and see if your current skill set is a good match or if you will require further training after you arrive.

For instance, if a person is contemplating moving to British Columbia (BC) where there is a high demand for truck drivers and you would like to get one of these driving jobs, you will need a Class 1 Driver's License in order to do so.

It would work in your favor if you have experience driving large trucks or semis prior to moving to BC, because the cost of driving lessons can range from seven to ten thousand dollars ($7000 - $10,000), give or take. If you already know how to drive a truck, then you can easily familiarize yourself with the theoretical aspects of driving in Canada (rode codes and laws) and go straight into doing the driving test to get the license you need. Transferrable skills are essential to making your job search less difficult.

Additionally, not all occupations are open to immigrants with just a work permit. A work permit holder who is a Medical Practitioner or Engineer in their home country for example, will not be able to get a job in that field when they arrive in Canada. This is owing to the fact that some occupations are regulated by the government and individuals are required to have Canadian certification or licensing in order to undertake employment in certain fields.

You may also need to sit mandatory federal or provincial government examinations before you are allowed to work in particular fields such as medicine, engineering, insurance and finance, to name a few.

To find out if your occupation is regulated or non-regulated, visit the following website:

https://www.cicic.ca/928/find_out_if_your_occupation_is_regulated_or_not.canada

Your job search will take a lot of time and effort especially being an immigrant. Although I was equipped with an MBA in International Business which I did in South Korea, I had to take a job at Walmart, which paid the minimum wage ($12.65/hour at the time). Thankfully, my salary was enough to cover our household necessities (rent, utilities and groceries).

Was this job what I desired? – Not at all. However, not only did it cover the necessities, but it also provided me with good experience, improved my time and money management skills, helped me plan better and adjust to the lifestyle and cost of living. This is the reality for the majority of new immigrants.

What we have to understand also is, the systems in Canada are different from what we are accustomed to and require re-learning and adaptation. Might I add, even Canadians are sometimes frustrated with the new systems being implemented by the government for citizens to access services. Being adaptable is a necessary life skill that is central to surviving and thriving in Canada.

Last, but certainly not least, is how Résumés and cover letters are written; this is another issue for immigrants. We make the mistake of sending out fancy CVs which don't work well for a job search in Canada. What is needed instead are functional, well-structured Résumés and straight-to-the-point cover letters. Most immigrants aren't told what is required for a job search prior to arrival, hence, many fall short when attempting to enter the labor market.

There is a learning curve which must be traversed before we get to the point of landing the ideal job in Canada. We also must take into consideration how transferrable our skills are. A functional Résumé should list your most relevant hard skills, employment history and your education/training.

Do not waste useful real estate on listing soft skills (unless that is all you have to offer) because everyone will claim to have the same soft skills.

Use the space instead, to differentiate yourself as much as possible and highlight the things that you do best.

A lot of research must be done when we consider immigration and many persons fall short here. Employment opportunities, labor market accessibility, employer openness, wages, etc. vary from province to province. "It's not an easy road" so we just have to do what we have to do and take nothing for granted. The good thing is, help is available, just ask for it.

Here's a big one that people often miss – NETWORKING. In your job search, never underestimate the value of networking. If you are not a 'people person', learn how to become one, and fast. There is such a thing called a hidden job market, which is best revealed through networking. In British Columbia for instance, it is believed that approximately eighty percent (80%) of the jobs are filled through networking. Simply put – people talk to people. The good thing is, you don't need to be close buddies from high school and you don't need a lot of money to do it.

In many Canadian cities, the local city council, private companies, charities, interest groups and chambers of commerce, host after-work networking events for a low entry fee or free of charge. These events bring together all kinds of professionals from all walks of life.

From entrepreneurs, managers, computer geeks, sports enthusiasts to CEOs, meeting the right person can go a long way in not just making settling easier, but can be assets to your future career pursuits in Canada. Check around, visit the city's official website, listen to the radio, check Facebook for events near you and visit your local employment services center to get information on these key events. Employment Service Centers can also help you with creating or updating your Résumé and cover letter.

The Job Bank is one of the best places to search for available employment opportunities across Canada prior to and after you arrive. Here is an excellent tool to conduct your job search:

https://www.jobbank.gc.ca/jobsearch/advance dsearch

To learn more about migrating to Canada for work, visit the following website:

https://www.canada.ca/content/dam/ircc/migr ation/ircc/english/pdf/pub/workbook-national.pdf

Point to note:

The best time of year to search for work is Spring (around April). Recruitment by employers generally slows as the weather gets colder, and almost grinds to a halt during Winter. Timing is key.

Sample Functional Résumé for job searching in Canada

Derville Lowe

123-19810 Doitright Ave., Abbotsford, BC, V3G 2X4

derville.lowe@gmail.com | 250-899-0000

Professional Summary/Skills/Highlights (Choose one)

- Over 10 years' experience in the [Banking Industry] ...
- Demonstrated track record in [sales] with a 90% growth rate...
- Trained and evaluated...
- Managed...
- Highly proficient in ...
- Performed...
- Developed and Implemented...
- Strong decision making, interpersonal, presentation, planning skills
- Achieved...

> Use keywords which best describe your key skills and experience; clearly making you the solution to the company's problem

Employment History

Job Title   July. 2019 - Present
Company, City, Province/State/Country
- Short job description – preferably 2 to 4 bulleted lines with key duties/achievements

Job Title   from/to Date
Company, City, Province/State/Country
- Short job description – preferably 2 to 4 bulleted lines with key duties/achievements

Job Title   from/to Date
Company, City, Province/State/Country
- Short job description – preferably 2 to 4 bulleted lines with key duties/achievements

Education & Training

Bachelor of Arts in Management   2009
Infinity University, City, Country

Any Other Degree/Certificate   2008
Institution Name, City, Country

Achievements (Optional)

Targets met
Results achieved
Improvements made
If any professional awards – justify awards with results

References available upon request

CHAPTER **NINE**
Studying in Canada
-

Canada has a robust, diverse, multi-cultural and dynamic international student population which sees students coming from all corners of the globe to pursue higher education at Canadian colleges and universities. The is due to Canada's world-class academic institutions, education system and the opportunities which are potentially available after graduation.

The value of international students to Canada's economy is significant, accounting for several billion dollars in revenue annually. According to a study conducted by Global Affairs Canada – Roslyn Kunin & Associates, Inc. on the *"Economic Impact of International Education in Canada"* (December 2017) – "the total annual expenditures of international students, including their visiting families and friends, contributed $12.8 billion and $15.5 billion to economic activities in Canada in 2015 and 2016, respectively." How about that for some perspective.

Most international students opt to remain in Canada as foreign workers after completing their studies and eventually become permanent residents and citizens. The process of transitioning from student to worker is fairly simple, since immigrant graduates are eligible for a one-time Post Graduate Work Permit (PGWP) after they complete their respective program of study.

If you plan on immigrating to Canada as a student, you should ensure that your preferred institution of study is a Designated Learning Institution (DLI). A DLI is an academic institution that is approved by the Government of Canada to host and provide training and certification to international students.

For more information on Designated Learning Institutions, please visit the following website:

https://www.canada.ca/en/immigration-refugees-citizenship/services/study-canada/study-permit/prepare/designated-learning-institutions-list.html

You don't need to pay high fees for consultancy in search of an opportunity to study in Canada. Save yourself the additional expense and make your study application a DIY project. An online search for Canadian colleges is quite easy, straightforward and really does not take a lot of effort.

Using the list of Designated Learning Institutions (DLI) is probably the best place to start your search for a college or university in Canada. This way, you will be certain that your selected institution has been accredited to offer training and issue certificates or degrees to international students. My advice to you is – take this route; you will be happy you did.

In your selection of a college or university, applicants are encouraged to check admission requirements, all applicable costs, school policy for international students, relevant payment schedules for tuition and fees, deadlines, accommodation for international students, available international bursaries and scholarships, English Language requirements, etc. This is crucial information for prospective students to know prior to applying. It will help with a smoother transition, minimize mistakes and frustration and help prospective students avoid unexpected expenses.

Once you get the necessary ground work done in terms of choosing your academic institution, you simply need to follow the instructions on the institution's website on how to apply. Most, if not all colleges and universities in Canada, accept applications through an online portal, so remember to scan all the required documents and have them ready to upload.

Using the guidelines provided, complete your application, provide supporting documents, pay your application fee, then submit your application.

Once the school makes a decision – which is most likely a favorable one – you will receive an official letter of acceptance. ***Your acceptance letter will be the most important piece of documentation you need in order to apply for a study visa.***

Next you need to prepare all the required documents to apply for your study visa.

Information and guidelines to assist you with applying for your visa can be found on the following website:

https://www.canada.ca/en/immigration-refugees-citizenship/services/study-canada/study-permit/

You don't need to worry about what supporting documents you need to provide with your visa application. A checklist showing all the relevant documents you need to prepare will be provided.

Once you have the documents ready, all you need to do is make an appointment at the nearest Visa Application Center (VAC) and submit your application package for a study visa. The staff at the

VAC will check your application package for completeness and provide any assistance you may need.

You are generally be required to pay your visa application fee at a designated bank and present the receipt of payment with your application. Preparing your visa application package will take a bit of time but it is a pretty straightforward process.

You can locate your nearest VAC on the following website:

https://www.vfsglobal.ca/Canada/

It is important that you have a concrete source of funding to cover tuition fees and living expenses, as well as proof of your funding source. Proof of funding is usually in the form of a letter of confirmation that you have been offered a scholarship, grant, bursary or sponsorship; OR an official bank statement from a registered financial institution, bearing your name or the name of your parent or guardian (if you are a minor).

The bank statement should show an account balance that is sufficient to cover the cost of your tuition and fees, travel and living expenses for yourself and your family (if applicable).

The amount should be sufficient to cover all your estimated expenses for at least one year.

Assuming your application for a study visa is successful, the rest of the preparation is pretty straightforward. Check in with your college or university and confirm the relevant dates for orientation and registration; confirm living arrangements; pack your bags; book your ticket and get ready for your 'big move'. You are about to embark on a new and exciting chapter of your life. A big change is coming.

Point to note:

*Once you land in Canada, please ensure that you **do not leave the airport** without receiving your study permit (remember, your visa IS NOT your permit). If you are not sure how to do this, please ask an officer from the Canada Border Services Agency (CBSA) at the airport for assistance and directions.*

It is crucial that you remember this as it will save you time and the headache, which will come with trying to obtain one after the fact.
DO NOT FORGET.

CHAPTER **TEN**
Child & Health Care

-

Persons who are moving to Canada with small children who will need day care, are encouraged to do a bit more research into the cost of child care in their destination province or city. Child Care in Canada is an expensive endeavor and should be carefully planned and budgeted for.

Of course, prior to moving to Canada, parents are required to provide proof of sufficient funds to show that they will be able to take care of themselves and their children. Let's say you pass that stage and you arrive in Canada and finally settle in; you will realize very quickly that child care is no child's play but is very costly. Child care services is also in high demand and this drives up the costs. The demand is so high in provinces like British Columbia and Ontario, that there are waiting lists for day care services. This can be very frustrating and challenging for working parents.

I don't know how better to say this, but plan as best as you can for the care of your young ones. In some cases, one parent may have to stay home for some time while arrangements are made for the children.

In cases where both parents are present in the home and both are employed, the work schedule has to be worked out in a way that allows one parent to work during the daytime and the other at night, if possible. Although this kind of arrangement is not ideal, it cannot be avoided in many cases due to the high cost and the unavailability of spaces at registered child care facilities.

Before you select a facility to send your toddler, it is recommended that you check reviews online and do your own research. Once you arrive in Canada and you find a place to live, do your best to check in with other parents in your neighborhood for assistance. Knock on a door and ask for help; it is highly likely that your neighbor will know and have useful tips and advice.

Reaching out for help is recommended as Canadians are generally open to having conversations with complete strangers. This type of networking in your community will prove very helpful in more ways than one.

I recommend a lot of research goes into this aspect. Also check the official website of your destination province, they usually have useful information for new immigrants with family.

Are you an immigrant parent? Here are a couple of great sources of information for immigrant parents and child care:

https://www150.statcan.gc.ca/n1/pub/89-652-x/89-652-x2014005-eng.htm

https://findingqualitychildcare.ca/

In addition to child care, there is also the matter of schooling. Selecting an appropriate academic institution for your child or children require prudence, proactivity, timeliness and financial readiness. If you are parents with minors and planning to immigrate with family, you should check the school district(s) in your destination city to get an idea of the number of schools appropriate for the age of your children. When making your choice for a school district, you should do so in relation to your place of residence.

Once you have made a choice, check the availability of space, enrollment and registration requirements and all associated costs, such as, tuition, fees, extracurricular activities, school equipment, bussing, etc. This will give you an estimate of what schooling will cost and help you budget and better prepare to meet your financial obligations.

For more information on school districts and elementary and secondary education in Canada, please visit the following websites:

https://www.canada.ca/en/immigration-refugees-citizenship/services/new-immigrants/new-life-canada/enrol-school/elementary-secondary.html

https://www.justlanded.com/english/Canada/Canada-Guide/Education/Public-Schools

Health Care

One of the most important aspects of living in Canada is health care. Canada has one of the best health care systems in the world and having good health insurance coverage is essential and must not be ignored. Health Insurance is generally provided by the Provincial Government as well as privately operated insurance companies. The type of health insurance coverage you get depends on your individual needs.

The Government of Canada offers publicly funded or subsidized health insurance which is accessible by obtaining a government-issued personal healthcare ID card and paying a relatively low monthly fee which is usually deducted from your income.

International Students are usually offered health insurance as a part of their registration package by the institution in which they are enrolled. For married students, this coverage often extends to the spouse of the student for an additional fee. This is convenient and removes the hassle of personally sourcing a health insurance plan.

Generally speaking, many employers partner with private insurers to offer optional extended health insurance coverage as a part of your benefits package. This is usually a cost sharing arrangement between employer and employee, where both parties each pay an agreed amount. The employee's contribution is typically deducted from their monthly or bi-weekly salary.

When you obtain employment, your employer will generally offer extended health care insurance coverage through a third-party insurer. Some employers offer a hundred percent coverage, while others have a cost sharing arrangement between employer and employee. Where the cost is shared, both parties contribute an agreed amount, with the employee portion being a pre-authorized deduction from their salary.

In cases where an employer does not offer health insurance coverage, individuals must independently seek coverage and make the necessary arrangements for the required monthly cost to be paid. Payments are usually done via electronic withdrawal or direct deposit. Having health insurance will significantly reduce very expensive up-front medical costs or even remove them altogether when you require medical attention.

Another issue which immigrants are usually unprepared for is the difficulty in finding a personal doctor or family physician. Most medical doctors have a full patient load and even have a waiting list for new patients. This is a common phenomenon in many cities across Canada. One solution to this is to seek medical attention at a Walk-In Clinic and develop a relationship with a doctor there. You can also try to get a referral from an acquaintance or friend, if possible.

Walk-In Clinics usually provide great health care and are sufficient to address general health concerns. You may also use the services offered here to get a sick note for work or school when proof of illness is required for absenteeism or sick leave. Sustained or prolonged medical care will require you to be registered with a family physician who will create a file of your medical history and make referrals for lab work and other specialized or extended care.

It is usually after being registered with a family physician can a person be referred to hospitals or to a specialist for further treatment, if necessary. Of course, there are exceptions to this, such as in emergency situations.

For more information on healthcare and Canada's healthcare system, please visit the following websites:

https://www.canada.ca/en/health-canada/services/canada-health-care-system.html

https://www.canada.ca/en/immigration-refugees-citizenship/services/new-immigrants/new-life-canada/health-care-card.html

Point to note:

Based on the high demand for child care services, if child care is your specialty or interest, it is a lucrative industry in which you can consider starting a business. When you are settled in and become acclimatized, just go ahead and find out what licensing you need. Also do your market research, check regulatory guidelines and get to work on that business plan.

Operating a child care facility in Canada is challenging and requires careful planning, but also very rewarding if you do it right.

CHAPTER **ELEVEN**
Financial Matters

-

Money management is a key skill to living in Canada and must be given careful attention. Life in Canada requires building a credit score and the best way to do this is to get and manage a credit card. Once you have a job, you should consider getting a credit card and use it to make some of your purchases online or at point-of-sale. The principle to managing your credit card is to ensure that you have adequate cash flow to clear your balance before the due date. If you do not clear your entire balance before the due date, you will incur a high interest penalty.

The best thing to do is to transfer the full amount you spent from your debit account to your credit account to clear the balance on the credit card. At best, ensure you pay more than your minimum monthly payment before or on the due date in order to avoid additional charges.

Many persons, including myself, have fallen into the trap of the convenience that having a credit card brings, without considering the fiscal responsibility that comes with it. Failure to properly manage your credit card is not only costly, but can negatively affect your credit score and result in unwanted debt. Please be diligent in handling this matter.

In your personal banking, overdraft protection is a good thing to have on both credit and debit accounts in case of emergencies or incidental expenditure, because they will come. While it may be good, you should avoid tapping into it as best as you can. We all know our own spending habits, so if you know you cannot manage an account with overdraft attached, please don't get it.

In order to keep a good credit score and avoid interest charges, do your best not to max out your credit card and always try to have at least half of your credit limit payed off at all times. It is also a good practice to pay on your credit card account before the due date, both you and your bank will be happy you did.

Endeavor to have savings as best as you can. I am not an avid saver, to be honest, but I have grown to appreciate its importance and have made it a point of practice. As is often said – 'life happens', and some expenses come unexpectedly. Hence, it is always good to be prepared for them when they arise. Canadian banks offer a Tax-Free Savings Account (TFSA) and other investment tools which allow you to put aside a set amount per month from your income. Make inquiries at your bank regarding how they work and chose the best one for you.

When shopping, look out for deals and take full advantage of coupons where available, especially if you shop frequently. Redeeming coupons in store or online will save you a few dollars. Ask about available discounts and negotiate prices wherever you can. If you are buying items such as perfume or make-up, ask for samples and get more value for your money. Product testing is highly recommended if available and will allow you to make better purchasing decisions.

Going out to have a good time with family or friends is always a needed break, but try not to eat out too much and practice cooking at home instead. Cooking at home saves money, the food quality unquestioned and it is much healthier. Additionally, you will know exactly what you are putting in your body.

You will find that the food you prepare at home is not just healthier, but tastier and more satisfying than what you'll pay a fortune for at that popular hot spot. When going to school or work, just pack a lunch kit, you will be happy you did.

Tax Tips

Upon arrival in Canada you are considered a 'resident' for tax purposes or a tax resident. Tax season in Canada can be the most rewarding or most disheartening time of year depending on how well you prepare. It is really up to you. When filing your taxes (usually between February and May), you should submit receipts of charitable donations along with the required T4 form. These are all used in assessing your tax returns. In the event you come up short and find yourself in arrears to the government, the assessment of the receipts from your donations will help to lower or even cover the amount you owe. As far as tax returns are concerned, giving is rewarding; call it good karma.

Many persons opt to undertake a part-time job in addition to their full-time. If you decide to work for more than one employer, it is advised that you ask your second employer to deduct approximately thirty percent (30%) of your income to go towards your income tax payments. This will prevent you being in arrears to the government after your tax return assessment is complete.

It is better to be prepared and have your bases covered from the onset than to be caught unawares. Doing this prevents a lot of frustration, especially if you had made plans for your tax returns, such as, paying bills, paying down a credit balance, school fees, visiting home, traveling, shopping, investing and saving. I am sure we would all love to be collecting rather than paying out at this time. It is better to be safe than sorry.

Owing taxes to the government is usually an unexpected expense and often comes at a time when people are looking forward to getting their tax returns. Many unsuspecting persons are thrown a curveball when informed that they are the ones who need to pay. Please do your best to avoid this situation and do not let that person be you.

Your part-time job may not be as rewarding if the necessary steps are not taken to prevent falling short in paying your taxes.

There are usually two options to file taxes – either do a self-assessment using a software package such as TurboTax or go the traditional route of using a reputable accounting company. The latter is safer if you are not sure how to go about filing for yourself and it will not cost you much.

Take the necessary steps to get your taxes done on time and make sure all your figures are correct. If you change your address at any time, please ensure that you update the Canada Revenue Agency (CRA) as soon as possible.

Prior to departing your home country for Canada, it is strongly advised that you obtain a record of employment or pay stubs from your employer for the months you worked in the current year, up to the time you leave. For instance, if you are moving to Canada in August, you should obtain your record of employment for January to July of the same year. This documentation will be used in your tax assessment in the ensuing year.

For your convenience, you should create an online account with the CRA to facilitate easy access to your tax assessments; get relevant information on taxation in Canada; manage electronic correspondence and receive relevant updates.

For more information on financial matters and taxation in Canada, please visit the following websites:

https://www.canada.ca/en/immigration-refugees-citizenship/services/new-immigrants/new-life-canada/plan-finances.html

 https://www.canada.ca/en/revenue-agency.html

Point to note:

The government usually announces exact dates and deadlines for filing taxes. Be on top of your taxes from early, it will save you a lot of time, frustration and of course, money.

CHAPTER TWELVE

Buying a Car

-

Living in certain parts of Canada, especially in places with infrequent or poor public transit, will require you to have a car. Before you leave for Canada, you can start making the determination as to whether you will need a car or not. This really depends on the part of the city or municipal district where you will reside.

Persons moving to smaller cities or townships may need a personal car, owing to the lack of reliable public transportation and the high cost of taxi services. On the flip side, larger cities tend to have reliable public transit such as, buses, trains and subway/commuter train. While having a car is convenient, it can be impractical for large cities due to traffic congestion and expensive parking charges.

The question then is – what should you do? I recommend checking your potential residence and look at public transit routes and schedules. Then, ascertain the cost of taxi services and look at the distance between home and work/school. With this information in mind, shop around and check the market for a car you can afford (A used car is recommended; they are usually in good condition). You will find that there are many options.

You should then check the cost of insurance, fuel and maintenance. Next, compare the cost of public transit (taxi, bus, train) per month with the monthly expenditure of owning a car. Some persons love the smell and feel of a new car – DO NOT BUY ONE. Wait and avoid taking on unnecessary debt.

If the cost of buying a car far exceeds using public transportation, then use the latter. If not, go ahead and buy that car, you will enjoy the convenience and freedom in owning one. Also, if you are an outdoors person, this may factor into whether you want to use public transit or get a car, since you will have the freedom of doing that road trip whenever you feel like it.

Sometimes convenience trumps everything else, but the reality of owning a car also comes with responsibility. Financing a car, even a pre-owned one, is expensive. It is better to be debt-free than to be servicing a high-interest car loan for half of a decade or more. Instead of financing a car, explore the plethora of options which are available from Used Car Dealerships. These cars are usually in good overall condition and have a much lower price tag.

You can plan on spending about three to four thousand dollars ($3000 - $4000) to buy a car in good working condition. The beauty of buying a car for cash is that you have full ownership with no lien or monthly payments to worry about; and you can sell or trade it in at any time with no encumbrances.

The only costs you will be concerned with are insurance, fuel and maintenance. Additionally, you can get your motor vehicle insurance premium lowered if you obtain an official driver's abstract or record from your insurance company in your home country. This documentation may seem insignificant but it can decrease your insurance premium by as much as ten percent (10%).

When car shopping, be very careful when you walk into a car dealership and you are treated especially well by that wonderful sales person. The job of a sales person is to sell, with no consideration for what you can really afford. In their selling, you will be the most special person in the world – or so it will seem. Be vigilant, keep your ears open and listen carefully. Also ask many questions and DO NOT FORGET to read the fine prints. It is your responsibility to ensure that you fully understand all the details, all the costs involved and get a full picture of the offer being made, before you accept and sign the motor vehicle sales agreement.

When offered warranties, please double check to ensure that it is or will be beneficial to you at some point within the warranty period, if at all. Warranty packages can be tricky and are sometimes disguised as benefits and sold to the buyer. These may only be of benefit to the dealership for them to earn extra money – be aware of this.

In our case, the dealership we went to sold us a lovely warranty package to cover 'anything' that may happen to our vehicle within the warranty period. It sounded beneficial so we accepted and paid an additional two thousand, five hundred dollars ($2500) on top of the cost of the car. We later discovered that the warranty only covered Tires and Rims (Really?!). Didn't I feel stupid. We fell for the nice sales pitch and hospitality and paid a high price for it. Do not let this be you.

Of course, we did not need that coverage at all, but we failed to check the details as we should have at the beginning. Checking the details of the contract when purchasing a car is imperative. DO NOT skip the details, remember to read through everything *(but still accept the free hot chocolate and snacks).*

Points to note:

Save yourself the trouble and additional expense by checking ALL the details of the sales agreement when purchasing a car. As they say – "the devil is in the details".

CHAPTER **THIRTEEN**
Renewing Permits

-

Your work or study permit is the most important piece of documentation for new immigrants. It serves as legal entitlement for the holder to carry out specified activities in Canada as a foreign worker or student. Your respective permit outlines the permissions and prohibitions and also grants access to various services and employment opportunities.

Many immigrants tend to become absorbed with their daily undertakings that they lose track of the time and completely forget that their permit is to be renewed. Do your best to ensure that you keep track of the time and do not forget the date that your permit will expire. You should apply to extend your permit and restore your status at least three (3) months before it expires, so that you receive the new one just before, or as soon as your current permit expires.

Your study or work permit has an expiry date, take note of it.

Your application for a new study or work permit is normally referred to as an 'extension of stay' or 'restoration of status' application. If you are unable to apply to extend your stay within the last three (3) months before your permit expires, you have ninety (90) days after your permit expires to remain in Canada and apply for a new permit. It is very unsettling to be in any foreign country without proper documentation and status and Canada is no exception, so it is important that you are on top of this particular aspect.

If you need help to get this done, please find a Regulated Canadian Immigration Consultant (RCIC) to assist you. An RCIC will ensure that your application meets the stipulations outlined by the Canadian Immigration Authorities. Of course, RCICs will charge a fee for this service. You may also seek assistance at any employment services center near you, free of charge.

The Government of Canada may decide to refuse your application to extend your work permit for any number of reasons, even if it makes no sense to you. When a permit application is refused, a portion of the fee you paid is normally refunded and you are given ninety (90) days from the date of your application refusal, to re-apply.

My work permit application was refused once, for a reason I found to be absurd but the situation was beyond my control. It is disheartening when this happens so it is very, very important that you keep track of this and ensure that you are prudent in submitting your application for your permit renewal on time; especially if you are a foreign worker.

If you find yourself in an unfavorable situation regarding your status or immigration matters and you have questions, you have the option of calling the ever-busy Immigration, Refugee and Citizenship Canada (IRCC) hotline to make inquiries. However, your chances of speaking with an IRCC representative will be slim to none and you will not be given the option to hold if the queue is full. Your best bet will be to utilize the information available online or seek help from an RCIC as mentioned earlier.

The fee I paid to apply for an extension of stay and restoration of status as a worker as at May 2019 was four hundred and fifty-five dollars ($455).

When my application was refused, I received a partial refund of three hundred dollars ($300), which was most welcomed considering the frustration I was experiencing at this point. Please give close attention to this subject and ensure you have the handle on it from the onset.

In essence, the portion of the fee that covers the work permit documentation is refundable but the application fee is not. Give close attention to this and ensure you have a full understanding.

For persons who are studying in Canada, you will be eligible for a Post-Graduate Work Permit (PGWP) upon completion of your course of study. The length of the PGWP will depend on the duration of your college or university program. Your PGWP will be issued once and cannot be renewed after it expires. Therefore, it is very important that you take the necessary steps to begin the process of applying for permanent residence in Canada as soon as possible.

The process of applying for Permanent Residence (PR) can be lengthy and tedious, hence, it is advised that you prepare the necessary documentation and get the process started early. Some of the things you will need to prepare for this include – language exam results, credential assessment, offer of employment (if applicable), academic certificate(s) and transcript(s), record of employment, etc.

Do not forget to check the applicable fees for your PR application, so that you can have the funds ready ahead of time. The amount of money you will need for this process depends on the pathway you opt to take.

Depending on your nationality, you may be required to do an English Language exam (e.g. IELTS) and have the results ready. Additionally, your credentials, such as certificates, diplomas or degrees may need to be assessed to ensure they meet Canadian standards or equivalency.

Please note that all the information, guidelines and forms you need are available online. Applications for permits and permanent residence can be submitted online by following a few simple steps to input the required information and attaching relevant documents. Simply follow the guidelines and instructions given on the respective website and systematically complete the application process.

If you have doubts and require assistance, Immigration Consultants and Lawyers will not turn you away, but be prepared to pay a sizable fee for their services.

Points to note:

Bear in mind that your provincial health care insurance plan will expire on the same date as your work/study permit. Therefore, it is important that your permit be renewed on time as this will also keep your health insurance active.

Immigration services are available through various immigration consultancy firms; however, you do not necessarily require such services. If you are not sure what do and need guidance, you may retain the services of a Regulated Canadian Immigration Consultant (RCIC) or immigration lawyer, to assist with renewing your permit, visa or any other type of immigration-related document or process.

CHAPTER **FOURTEEN**
Canada Post-COVID-19
-

To the COVID-19 frontline workers, I use this space to single you out and say a **BIG THANK YOU** for your selflessness and sacrifice! We see you. God sees you. We all appreciate you. You have big hearts, and your reward will be even bigger! **THANK YOU!**

To those of you who have lost love ones, neighbors, co-workers or friends, my deepest sympathies and prayers go out to you. Let us care for, share with, encourage and help each other in whatever way we can. We are all in this together and better days are ahead.

We have this hope.

♥

The COVID-19 Pandemic was the most unexpected, unsuspected, hard-hitting, life-changing, world-altering and most unimaginable event of 2020 and possibly the 20th century. It was unprecedented to say the least. Many lives and livelihoods were affected and so many lost.

We all experienced it in our own way, wherever we were in the world. It showed us how fragile we are and how much we need each other. It took a lot from us, but it also gave a lot – a lot of experiences and lessons that will last for generations to come.

We are grateful to God, despite the hardships we all faced. We are thankful for the gains – the many recoveries; the many family ties rekindled; the many evidences of kindness and outpouring of love; the testing and strengthening of faith; the many evidences of our resilience, comradery and ingenuity and the many sacrifices, especially those made by all the front-line workers all over the world.

With all the changes that have occurred since the Coronavirus outbreak, rules of travel and immigration have also changed for most, if not all countries.

If you are planning to immigrate to Canada after the government fully reopens the country to international students and workers, you will most likely need to get a medical examination done prior to traveling, to prove that you have not contracted the virus.

All governments around the globe, including Canada, have made comprehensive changes to international travel and immigration policy to protect against the spread of COVID-19. It is very important that you are aware of these changes prior to leaving your home country. The Canadian government has attempted to provide updates to the public regarding the changes it has made as a result of the pandemic. You are encouraged to do some reading in this respect.

Moving to Canada has always necessitated careful planning, but the emergence of COVID-19 has brought on higher levels of security and scrutiny. Be prudent about your planning and ensure that you are aware of any new guidelines and changes to immigration rules and follow them accordingly.

Adjusting to the New Normal

If you were accepted by an academic institution to study in Canada, please check in with your school to get information and updates regarding any changes in schedules, courses, enrollment, program delivery, etc. Most colleges and organizations have been providing frequent updates on their websites, so please ensure that you remain current with all the changes and stay on top of your preparation. Remaining current in this time and going forward, is crucial.

All across Canada, the government, schools, recreational facilities, shopping malls, business and other public spaces, have implemented changes to make the public and the workplace safer. Social distancing and remote work have become common place; and how you go about doing business has changed drastically. These changes will continue into the foreseeable future as measures are put in place to control the spread of the virus. Be prepared for these changes and be ready to adapt to the 'new normal'. Your ability to adapt quickly is even more crucial now more than ever.

When it comes to the labor market, many jobs are still available while others have moved to remote work. Working from home or another satellite location is no longer a perk of the job, but a requirement for many jobs. Many aspects of general life have gone virtual – from school rooms to boardrooms.

Use of Technology

If you are not very acquainted with using computers and other devices smart phones and tablets, I suggest you get the training you need to get up to speed with using them. Take the time to familiarize yourself with the various communication and document processing software, the internet, social media, video conferencing and email usage. These skills are now as crucial to your job as the clothes you wear to work – learn them.

Many *free* computer-related training courses are available online through various platforms and many tutorials can be found on YouTube. Take full advantage of them and upgrade your skills as you will need them.

Be Innovative and Adaptable

Despite the many setbacks caused by the COVID-19 Pandemic, many persons – myself included – have found themselves digging deeper and refining those under-utilized or buried skills and talents.
Personally speaking, practicing and refining my skills has been quite a rewarding experience.

My wife and I were both in different countries at the time of the outbreak – She was in London, Ontario (Canada) and I was in Homestead, Florida (USA).

We needed something that would occupy our time and keep us connected mentally while we were separated. We worked on several projects and this was when I started my own business – Norwood Creative Hub, a multimedia and creative content design company.

God gave me the idea for this company and I took off with it. Being unemployed at the time, it was the perfect time to throw all my energy into it. The business started taking shape while I was hunkered down during the height of the COVID-19 outbreak.

My wife, who always did drawings just for fun, became an expert illustrator in her own right. With her illustrating skills, coupled with my writing and design skills, we worked together to create books, merchandize and content for kids under the 'Just Genios' brand which I conceptualized.

We have since created and published two awesome books for toddlers – "Just Genios Animal ABCs" – an interactive alphabet learning and activity book and "Just Genios Animal 123s" – an interactive counting book. This was not a part of our 2020 plans, but God gave us the inspiration and, despite the setbacks and being physically separated, we worked together to create something fantastic.

When you arrive in Canada and get settled, it is the perfect time to try out your ideas and explore the possibilities. You never know what will happen until you try something different. Learning and trying new things in Canada is pivotal to your growth and generating income. Be ready to learn, make changes and adapt to the changing environment.

Going into business in Canada is common place for immigrants – from small local shops to medium-sized and even large nationwide businesses. Approximately eighty (80) percent of British Columbia's labor market is based on entrepreneurship. If you choose to go into business, do some market research, create a business plan and be aware of market trends and consumer behavior.

The business landscape has changed drastically due to COVID-19, including spending habits, demand for certain consumer goods, business operations and there has been a significant increase in the use of online retail and service offerings. If your business will involve physical contact and the gathering of people, such as a restaurant, coffee shop or café, beauty salon, clothing store, etc., be aware of the new rules for operating such businesses. You will need to be aware of the new rules of engagement and ensure that you implement them for your own protection and that of your customers and employees.

With a seemingly never-ending list of things to do and critical decisions to make as a result of the pandemic, it is imperative that you are organized and have all the right information as you get yourself ready for this next chapter of your life.

If you are a parent and immigrating with minors, preparation is even more crucial. You will not just need to manage the necessary details for yourself, but must also ensure that all the relevant essentials are in place to secure your child or children, in order to avoid encumbrances either at the application or immigration stage.

In all things, preparation is key. It is said that the only thing constant is change – ***prepare*** for it.

MAP OF CANADA

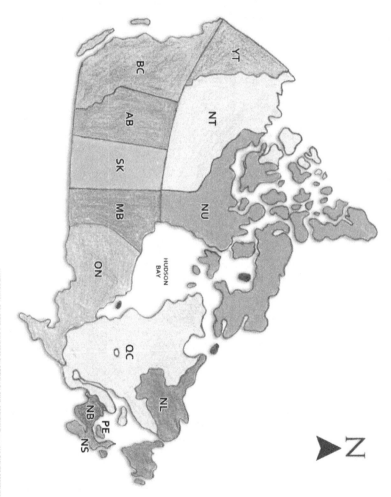

PROVINCES AND TERRITORIES OF CANADA

Official websites shown

Provinces

Name	Abbr.	Website
Alberta	AB	http://www.albertacanada.com
Manitoba	MB	http://www.immigratemanitoba.com
Saskatchewan	SK	http://www.saskatchewan.ca
New Brunswick	NB	http://www.welcomenb.ca/
British Columbia	BC	http://www.welcomebc.ca
Quebec	QC	http://www.immigration-quebec.gouv.qc.ca
Ontario	ON	http://www.ontarioimmigration.ca
Prince Edward Island	PE	http://www.gov.pe.ca/immigration/
Nova Scotia	NS	http://novascotiaimmigration.ca/
Newfoundland and Labrador	NL	http://www.nlimmigration.ca

Territories

Yukon	YT	http://www.immigration.gov.yk.ca/
Nunavut	NU	http://www.gov.nu.ca/
Northwest Territories	NT	http://www.gov.nt.ca/

- 101 -

REACH OUT TO THE AUTHOR
with your feedback, queries and requests for signing & bookings

-

derville.lowe@gmail.com

OTHER BOOKS BY THIS AUTHOR

Just Genios Animal ABCs: *An Interactive Learning and Activity Book*

TITLE AVAILABLE ON AMAZON

Just Genios Animal 123s: *An Interactive Counting Book (Multilingual – English, Español, Français)*

TITLE AVAILABLE ON AMAZON

Made in the USA
Columbia, SC
27 December 2020